THE JOY OF

BEING A

CATECHIST

THE JOY OF
BEING A
CATECHIST

From Watering to Blossoming

GLORIA DURKA, Ph.D.

Resurrection Press
Mineola • New York

"Dreams," on p. 37, is from *The World Tomorrow,* 1923, cited in *Langston Hughes* by James A. Emanuel (New York: Twayne Publishing, 1967).

"Ode to the Dodo," on p. 40, is from *Collected Poems 1953–1987* by Christopher Logue (London: Turret Books, 1987).

"The Grandeur of God," by Gerard Manley Hopkins, on p. 48, is cited from *The Oxford Book of English Mystical Verse* (Oxford: Clarendon Press, 1953).

The parable on p. 49 is cited from *Song of the Bird* by Anthony De Mello (New York: Doubleday, 1982).

All scripture quotes are from Good News Bible–Catholic Study Edition (New York: Sadlier, 1976).

First published in 1995 by Resurrection Press, Ltd.
P.O. Box 248
Williston Park, NY 11596

Second printing – December, 1995
Third printing – May, 1996
Fourth printing – September, 1996

Cover design by John Murello

Printed in the United States of America.

To Sister Mary Annette Guzowski, CSSF
educator, leader and visionary
on the occasion of her 101st birthday

YOU ARE WRITTEN IN OUR HEARTS
BY THE SPIRIT OF THE LIVING GOD
(2 Cor 3:3)

Contents

7

FOREWORD

If you have decided to retire from being a catechist and have said to yourself and maybe to others, "I think I've served my time — let others take over," or, if after a particularly hard year you've promised yourself that you'll never teach again, do not, DO NOT, we warn you, read this book. Put it behind you right now! If not, you may end up changing your mind.

On the other hand, if you're toying with the possibility of volunteering to be a catechist, sit right down and read it. The first chapter, alone, will convince you that you're about to embark on something that will be significant, worthwhile, good not only for others, but also for you, personally and spiritually. That is not to say that the task is easy nor that the commitment you're making won't be, at times, costly. It's merely saying that catechizing is a vital ministry that you may not want to miss being part of. That's what this book says in a truly believable, beautifully poetic way.

The second chapter is amazing in how it pinpoints precisely who we are as catechists: "people who answer the call of the community to be instruments of instruction, formation and transformation." The hallmark of that chapter, for us, is what it says about why catechists should not only care about their students but should care about caring. The author's wisdom is revealed in this sentence, "Youngsters 'grow and glow' if they experience care." We find her wisdom and experience believable because at one of the closing events with the 7th graders that we taught recently, some of the young people hugged us spontaneously. And as we walked to our car, we knew that besides teaching, we had done well what Dr. Durka emphasizes in this chapter — we had cared for and about each one individually as well as part of a group. When we respond to the call to be catechists we have the wonderful opportunity to feed the hunger for care in those we are catechizing.

Lest, in spite of being almost sure that you can meet the challenge of caring, and like Dr. Durka are convinced that "Teaching is an amazing grace," but you're still worried about the particulars of what to teach, Chapter Three is a real consoler. First, the chapter reminds us that there is plenty of help available to us and second, that what we're doing is only one important piece of a rich tapestry. We are simply "building on the foundation of what the children received earlier, as well as laying that foundation deeper and wider for what will follow in subsequent years." And that foundation includes the guidance and formation of family and the other institutions of society.

Our favorite of all five chapters of this splendid volume is the fourth because it deals so well with imaging ourselves, imaging God and helping students with their images of self. A healthy self image makes it possible to believe that we are, indeed, the *Imago Dei*. Our students, influenced by our healthy image, may have a greater chance of seeing themselves as *Images of God.*

Helps are given in this chapter for image building in ourselves as well as in our students. It's a most practical chapter that closes with a delightful and memorable parable.

As we finished the fifth and final chapter we were deeply moved, partly because of a story that Dr. Durka shares out of her own experience, but also because of what the chapter says of who we are as catechists. In essence, that chapter sums up the whole book. Dr. Durka identifies catechists as ministers and goes on to define ministry, "as doing something in public, for the coming of the reign of God, on behalf of the community;

it is a grace, and it has its own identity and structure." That's a nearly perfect definition of catechetical ministry in a nearly perfect book. We're certain that any cate-chist about to become an ex-catechist will have second thoughts upon reading this volume, any catechists who are continuing, will be motivated and inspired, and any who are considering the vocation will most likely answer the call.

This book is wonderful and we recommend that it be given to every catechist and/or potential catechist as a gift before or at the first in-service meeting of the parish.

JANAAN MANTERNACH, D. MIN.
CARL J. PFEIFER, D. MIN.

Catechists and Co-authors of
Catechetical Materials

INTRODUCTION

Every day throughout the land thousands of people just like you set about to do something amazing — they take time from their busy lives to serve their parishes as catechists.

Life for most people is spent doing a lot of ordinary things. The ordinary is limited, but there are some in the community who are called to see the extraordinary in the ordinary. Catechists are such people. In your teaching, by your words and example, you are helping others to have glimpses of grace amidst the ordinariness of everyday life. And what is equally wondrous is that in doing this work of catechesis, you find that teaching can feed different layers of your own soul.

It is my hope that in some small measure this little work can help you to be aware that all of us together are watered with grace when we teach, and that **"like flowers of the field we blossom"** (Ps 103:15).

One

THE AMAZING GRACE OF TEACHING

Have you ever asked yourself, "Why am I doing this?" as you prepared to meet your class? If you have, then you are like most catechists. From time to time, we get bogged down with the sameness of a routine or feel drained from putting so much energy into preparing and presenting classes that are interesting as well as informative. We may feel as though our creative energies are being exhausted. In fact, we may feel that we are getting physically exhausted from the experience. Together with the psalmist, we might pray,

> I am worn out, O Lord; have pity on me!
> Give me strength; I am completely exhausted....

> (Ps 6:2)

And yet we keep at it because every now and then we see that our students "grow and glow" in the process of being catechized. Every now and then we have the experience of realizing that we are engaged in something wonderful, and that insight itself is enough to sustain us and "makes it all worthwhile." We are helping to build up the body of Christ:

> Christ gave some as apostles, and some as prophets, and some as evangelists, and some as pastors and teachers, for the equipping of the saints for the work of service, to the building up of the body of Christ.... (Eph 4:11)

As catechists we show our love by being willing to extend ourselves for the purpose of nurturing the spiritual growth of others as well as ourselves. Those who work with children and young people catechize in the hope that they will "be like plants that grow up strong" (Ps 144:12).

The Joys of Teaching _____

What, then, is teaching? It is an intentional act. We do it because we aim to communicate and instruct. Teaching doesn't occur accidentally; it is intended. Learning, however, can occur unintentionally. People learn from a variety of sources and in a variety of situations. Not so with teaching. A teacher is determined to instruct others. When a catechist teaches, she or he is concerned with proposing information, skills and criteria to the students. The information in catechesis consists of the heritage and tradition of the Christian community. Skills include how we live these out in our daily lives. The criteria include guides and guidelines for making responsible choices.

The activity of teaching religion helps to illuminate the Living God who is present in our midst. When we teach, we make the traditions of our religious community accessible, i.e., our rich heritage is made available to the students in a way that can make a difference in their lives. It includes an awareness and appreciation of the tradition of our Catholic community. And when we teach, we also make *manifest* the connection between knowing and living the tradition, and transforming our lives. That is to say that teaching helps students to tease out what the tradition means for their lives today. As catechists we make sure that *stories* of our heritage are attended to with care and understanding. These include stories of the lives of the saints — the holy women and men who came before us. By telling their stories we keep their memories alive. The tradition also includes the meaningful celebration of Christian life preserved through liturgy and the sacraments. Our instruction helps our students to more fully participate in them and to reflect on their meanings in our lives today. This suggests that teaching has transformative power as well. Through the prism of our past, reflected in the Bible, in the lives of the saints, in the sacraments, and in doctrine, we can see more clearly what must be transformed in our world today. As we deepen our realization of what we are participating in when we teach, we can experience great joy in recognizing that teaching is a vocation. We read of how unique this vocation is in the *Declaration on Christian Education,* published during the Second Vatican Council,

> Splendid, therefore, and of the highest importance is the vocation of those who help parents in carrying out their duties and act in the name of the community by undertaking a teaching career. This vocation requires special qualities of mind and heart, most careful preparation and a constant readiness to accept new ideas and to adapt to the old. (*Declaration on Christian Education,* 1965, no. 5)

These words of the Council Fathers suggest that teaching is ultimately directed towards new life, that is, toward infusing the community over and over again with new energy and vision.

But what does this mean for teachers? What kind of persons could possibly do all of this? Does it mean having a sparkling personality, or compelling charismatic gifts? While these could help, the source of vitality for the teacher is much more her or his deep-rooted spirituality. A good teacher, like the just person, is

> ... like a tree
> planted by streams of water
> that yields its fruit in due season,
> and its leaves do not wither.

(Ps 1:3)

The Challenge of Teaching ————————————

Let's be honest, too. Teaching *is* difficult. It has always been so. The scripture writer said so, centuries ago. In the Book of Isaiah, we read the following:

> You will indeed listen but never understand,
> and you will indeed look, but never perceive.
> For this people's heart has grown dull,

and their ears are hard of hearing,
and they have shut their eyes so that they might not
   look with their eyes,
and listen with their ears,
and understand with their heart and turn — and I
   would heal them.

(Is 32:14–15)

Does this passage seem to describe the occasional response of your classes? If so, you are not alone. Experienced teachers suggest that teaching is difficult, but that once we truly recognize this important truth, we can rise above it. This is to say that we can understand and accept that teaching is difficult so that it will no longer really disturb us. What will really matter is that we still wish to teach because we enjoy it.

We must feel good about teaching because feelings are the source of our energy. If we feel poorly, our energy is diminished. And here is a paradox. Vitality is connected with vulnerability. Because teaching is ultimately a deeply personal activity, it is filled with many small uncertainties. Even Jesus recognized how difficult it is to see so many of our carefully chosen words fall on rocky ground or get choked by weeds (recall the Parable of the Sower, Mk 4:1–9). It is not pleasant to have our impatience show, or to have others see that we are ignorant of certain things. And it is not easy to have to face our limited energy or to find our creativity being drained.

But, according to Christian tradition, power is made evident in weakness. When we feel weak, it is easier to remember the words of St. Paul:

> For what we preach is not ourselves, but Jesus Christ as Lord...we have this treasure in earthen vessels, to show that the transcendent power belongs to God and not to us.
>
> (2 Cor 4:5a, 7)

Recently, contemporary writers have suggested that in the Scriptures proclaiming the word of God often was paralleled with *ruah,* or spirit. Once spoken, it remained in existence, carrying out its activity indefinitely. It was never lost. It remained real, and it was endowed with the power of the one who spoke it. The words of Isaiah describe this *positive* power of teaching so well:

> Yes, as the rain and the snow come down from the
>   heavens
> and do not return without watering the earth,
> making it yield and giving growth

to provide seed for the sower and bread for the
   eating,
so the word that goes from my mouth
does not return to me empty,
without carrying out my will
and succeeding in what it was sent to do.

(Is 55:10–11)

The word of Yahweh cannot fail. As catechists, when we teach we share in this promise.

It can help to refresh us if we recall this promise, and to remember that Jesus sealed this promise again when he said, "It is to the glory of my Father that you should bear much fruit" (Jn 15:8).

For catechists, teaching *is* an amazing grace.

Here is one example of just how amazing teaching can be:

It was a bright fall day and the sun made the morning air feel just a bit warmer than what the thermometer read. Sister Miriam had just parked her car in the lot next to the church and was crossing the street when she noticed two young children sitting on the steps of the convent stoop. The two young boys were about six or seven years old, and it was obvious from their clothes that they were quite poor. "They must be some children from one of the outreach programs," Sister Miriam thought to herself as she drew nearer. But then it dawned on her very quickly that nothing was scheduled for that early in the morning, or at least she couldn't recall anything. A bit puzzled, she called out to the children, "Good morning little ones! What brings you out to St. Anthony's so early on a Saturday morning?" Looking up from their conversation, one of the boys quickly replied, "We are waiting for Sister Verna." And the second boy said, "I hope she comes *this* week!" Oh, said Sister Miriam, a bit stunned by their reply. "You mean you were waiting for Sister Verna last week, too?" "Sure," the first child replied. "We come here every Saturday morning for school with Sister." "Yeah," said the second child. "She teaches us about God, and we have lots of fun, too. But she must have forgotten the last couple of weeks because she never showed up." "I'll bet she'll come today," said the first child. "It's such a nice day and it will be a good one to go out looking for leaves like she promised." Sister Miriam swallowed and took a deep breath as she approached the boys. "Let's go inside, boys," she said. "I have something to tell you." As she opened the convent door, and stepped inside with the two youngsters, she whispered a prayer, "Please, Lord, help me to tell these children ever so gently that Sister Verna is not coming today nor any other day."

In spite of not being well, Sister Verna continued her teaching ministry right until the end. Her Saturday morning religion classes were pockets of joy in the lives of so many poor youngsters. The children laughed, sang, prayed, did art work, listened to stories and were loved by Sister Verna and they knew it. Although the parish was in dire need of resources, she somehow managed to gather all kinds of items that could be used in teaching religion.

Her creativity was amazing, and it seemed that she could find a use for almost anything. But what was the most astounding aspect of Sister Verna's teaching is how it impacted the lives of her students. Sister Miriam told me that for the next couple of months she would regularly come upon small groups of children who gathered at the convent steps to wait for Sister Verna. Even some who had received the news of her death continued to show up with the others in the hope that just maybe the grown ups were wrong, and just maybe, Sister Verna would have class today.

I tell this story because it is a splendid illustration of how catechists experience the challenge of teaching. Sister Verna had been my student for a few years, and I knew how she wrestled with self-doubt, and how she worried about her own limitations. Yet she was never paralyzed by these concerns. Her love and concern for the poor, especially the children, spurred her on to do what-ever she could to help them know the love of God in their lives. And they did, even though Sister Verna never stopped worrying about how she could do her work bet-ter. I can still recall her broad smile when she thought she was taking herself too seriously. "I guess I just have to do whatever I can," she would say, "and I'll trust God to take care of the rest." Good advice. It worked for her; it can work for all of us.

Reflection Questions —————————————

1. Why are you a catechist?

2. Think for a moment about the students you teach. What are some of the joys you experience when teaching them?

3. What are some of the difficulties?

4. Can you think of ways to minimize these difficul-ties?

5. Can you think of ways to maximize the joys?

Two

FEEDING HUNGERS

What do you think matters more to the people you know, having enough things, or having peace of mind? Or to put it another way, do you think that having lots of things will guarantee happiness? Sociologists of religion have suggested that in the United States we are experiencing a shift from materialism to simplicity of life. The decade of the '80s, they say, was characterized by the desire of people to accumulate wealth quickly and to spend it just as fast. Whereas, for more and more people the '90s seem to be years of returning to a simpler lifestyle in which spirituality is prized more than materialism. Put simply, people seem to be *hungry* for something more to life, and for a deeper way of living humanly.

A Catechist Is One Who Feeds
Hungers of the Heart _____

When catechists teach religion, they have one basic purpose, namely, *to create a milieu in which faith can be awakened, nourished, and challenged.* Catechists teach because of their faith. For Christians faith is a relationship of trust in God, and God's creation, that is, trust in self, others, and the world. God's loving kindness and faithfulness have been shown to us in Jesus the Christ; this is the heart and soul of Christianity.

Years ago, when we were very young, we learned that faith is a gift. Now as catechists it is helpful to remember that we cannot "cause" another person to have faith. But we can help to provide our students with a loving, caring environment in which growth in faith becomes a real possibility. Within this environment, the catechist guides students to grow in the relationship of trust in God by helping them to grow in at least four aspects of faith:

1. *beliefs* about God that serve as the basis of our trust

2. an ongoing, personal *relationship* with God that brings us into a relationship with other persons of faith

3. a *commitment* to God as trustworthy that shapes the way we invest our time and energy

4. an awareness of the *mystery* that surrounds God and places limits on our understanding and control of God

Of course, there are many other aspects of faith, such as obedience and service on behalf of the reign of God, but for catechists the four aspects given above are central to the task of catechesis. How we are instruments of helping our students to feed their hungry hearts is itself a mystery, as St. Paul reminds us: "People must think of us as Christ's servants, *stewards* entrusted with the mysteries of God" (1 Cor 4:1).

Feeding Hungers Requires Care _____

Why should a catechist care about caring? Because caring presumes that there is a fundamental relationship between the "one-caring" and the "cared-for." In the case of catechesis, the relationship between the catechist and the student is central to the teaching process. Nowhere is this more necessary than in catechesis of the young. Even though all of us need to know that we are "cared about," children and youth need *inclusion* and *confirmation* in the communities in which they live. Youngsters "grow and glow" if they experience care. The teacher (one-caring) encounters the student (cared-for) as a "Thou," in the language of Martin Buber, and not as "It," an object of analysis. The encounter between cate-chist and student is a catechetical moment which is full of hope and beauty.

Caring Must Be Nurtured _____

Psychologists tell us that children learn more by osmosis than by exhortation. This is to say that children absorb a great deal of learning from their environment. This ob-servation can be helpful to catechists because it reminds us that our own witness is a powerful teaching aid. We can model ways of caring in our own lives. A few ex-amples can be helpful. In our teaching, we can foster in students an *appreciation and affirmation of repetition.* This would include helping students recognize the sacred rhythms of human experience, such as the repetition of feelings and events in ordinary life, e.g., hunger, tired-ness, gladness, the coming of daylight, etc. We can show children that these repetitions are also promises which are fulfilled over and over again. And we can model for the children how we ourselves celebrate the ordinary rhythms of life with joy and delight. By so doing we are implicitly teaching that life is worth living, and living well — in faith.

Who Calls Us to Teach? _____

Some may wish to answer, "My pastor called me" or "The parish Director of Religious Education called me up and asked me to volunteer." Or perhaps some may truly feel called by the Spirit to personally get involved with the religious education program in the parish. While these details may be true, the ministry of teaching is never simply a personal or private affair. No matter whether one is recruited to teach, or whether one has a strong urge to teach, catechists teach because *the community calls us.* This community of the People of God understands itself as being in need of instruction, formation and transformation, and so it needs some members who will be instruments of instruction, formation and transformation. Catechists are persons who respond to the vocation, or calling, given by Jesus:

> You did not choose me,
> no, I chose you;

and I commissioned you
to go out and bear fruit,
fruit that will last. . . .

(Jn 15:16)

And that call is always to the community, the People of God.

In sum, then, catechists are those who feed hungers of the heart by praising God with all their heart, and by telling of all the wonderful things God has done! (Ps 9:1).

Reflection Questions ————————————————

1. What are some of the hungers of the heart that you find in your students?

2. How do you try to feed these hungers?

3. What are some of your own hungers of the heart?

4. How do you feed these?

Three

PLANTING ROOTS, GIVING WINGS

What am I doing? Have you ever asked yourself this question? Most of us have, and many times, at that. Fortunately, when it comes to teaching as a catechist, we don't have to be too concerned about the particulars of what to teach. We use materials that are designed to help us all along the way. There are textbooks with specific lessons for each class meeting. There are teacher guides that give us helpful background to the content that we will be teaching. There are specific suggestions for a variety of activities that can be used with the students. And there are usually supplementary materials such as videos, cassette tapes of songs, posters, and art supplies available through the parish or school resource center. Best of all, perhaps, is the realization that we do not have to do everything when it comes to educating our students. What we are doing is one important piece of a rich tapestry that includes the guidance and formation of family and the other institutions of society. Our teaching is one part of the larger fabric of the total curriculum that has been adopted for the religious education of children throughout their school years.

Our part fits into a larger whole, and as we work to do our best, we trust that what we are doing is building on the foundation of what the children received earlier, as well as laying that foundation deeper and wider for what will follow in subsequent years. We teach in the belief that we are passing on what we have already received, in the hope that those who receive it, will know it better than we have known it, so that this inheritance can be more deeply appreciated. As suggested in the previous chapter, we teach a living heritage that has been preserved for us not only through words, but through the lives of disciples, prophets and martyrs. This gift of our heritage is a *forming grace* that helps us to know who we are *spiritually,* that is, to *know our roots.*

Planting Roots ————————————————

Every one loves a good story. So do the students we teach. Stories can help us to learn where we came from, and they can point to where we are going. The stories of our tradition can make faith come alive for us in the present. They give us a sense of our history. Learning the stories of the women and men who lived Christian lives before us, can help us to act today. We can first look at our own lives and decide what must be done, and then look to the lives of the heroes before us to see if they can shed any light on how we can do what must be done. We derive inspiration and hope from history. Sometimes we are privileged to meet living heroes and heroines. Through them we make real contact with history. Here is one story about such an encounter. Only the names have been changed.

It was the first day of the fall semester at Immaculate Heart of Mary College. The usual buzz and excitement filled the corridors as students scurried from offices to classrooms. A few students had gathered early in the room assigned for the course, "Faith and Culture in Contemporary Society." A new professor was scheduled to teach this subject, and word was out that the class was "closed out," that is, filled to capacity. As a few early arrivals spoke to each other, other students slowly began to gather. In the midst of one group, there appeared a slender, elderly looking nun who was dressed in full habit. Could she be the new professor? Apparently not, as she took a seat near the middle of the room. As the scheduled hour drew near, the classroom quickly began to fill up. Perhaps the elderly nun was a visitor to the campus and was sitting in for today's session. "Good morning, and welcome," said a cheery voice. Obviously the teacher had arrived, a middle-aged woman who exuded professionalism and enthusiasm. After going over the course prospectus and answering some questions, the professor suggested that the class take a few moments for introductions. Each student took a turn giving their name and hometown and a brief statement of why she or he had chosen this course. When it came time for the elderly nun to take her turn, she surprised all by stating that now that she is retired, she is taking time to do some of the things she did not have time for while she worked at a full-time job. She told the students that while she was returning by bus from a pilgrimage to the shrine of Sainte Anne de Beaupré in Canada to celebrate her 90th birthday (a trip of about 400 miles!) she resolved to take a few college courses. And so here she was. "Besides," she said, "I enjoy being with young people." The students were stunned. What would it be like to have a 90-year old classmate, and a nun at that? The professor, a longtime acquaintance of mine, delighted in reporting to me that Sister Ann fit right in with the students. Most found it amazing to be in the company of such a bright, cheerful, and open-minded person. And they could not hear enough of her stories. In her person they met living history, and they experienced it through her eyes. Who can tally up all the stereotypes that were broken in this encounter of an elderly nun with thirty or more 20-year olds? Intergenerational exchange is enriching for the entire community, and in this instance, the course evaluations testified to how much the students learned about history and about *themselves* from their relationship with the wise woman in their midst. She certainly made Christian history come alive for them.

Developmental psychologists tell us that one of the chief tasks of youth is identity formation. Young people are in the process of discovering who they are, and when we teach religion to them, we are contributing to this process of identity formation. Based on the story of who we are as a Christian people, we are helping our students to know and embrace Christian values.

Are Values "Caught" or "Taught"? _____

Some of us will probably remember the popular slogan in educational circles of the '70s, "Values are caught, not taught." Almost a quarter of a century later, the slogan being uttered today is, "Values are caught *and* taught." We better understand what the earlier slogan was meant to convey, namely, that much learning is acquired through observation and imitation. In other words, what is implied by actions teaches more than what is explicitly stated in words. Remember the phrase, "actions speak louder than words?" Today we can better appreciate the relationship between actions and words. To put it another way, we recognize that indeed, values can be taught, too. When we teach the "content" segment of our lesson, we are transmitting the inheritance of our shared values. Through discussion and reflection we aim to help students make connections to their own lives, now, and to enable them to freely choose to *embrace* and *act* on Christian values that are given to us through Scripture and doctrine. So, ours is the responsibility to conserve and transmit the heritage of values we have received, so that those who come after us may receive this precious gift even more solid and secure than we have received it. In other words, when we teach, *we are planting roots.*

Giving Wings _____

> Hold fast to dreams
> For if dreams die
> Life is a broken-winged bird
> That cannot fly.

Hold fast to dreams
For if dreams go
Life is a barren field
Frozen with snow.

— Langston Hughes

We all have dreams, and we all need dreams. In this poem the author is suggesting that dreams are the stuff that hope is made of, and while this is true for all of us, it is especially true of young people. Youth are the promise of the future. When we educate the young, we are helping them to believe that life is worth living, and that their own lives will make a difference to life on this planet. The ability to hope, dream and imagine are uniquely human characteristics, and we are all born with that ability. Teachers are actually building on this inborn capacity. In fact, the word "education" comes from "_educere_," which translates as "to lead forth." So when we are educating, there is a real sense in which we are drawing out that which is already present. We are drawing out the hope and belief that the world can be made a better place. It can be transformed.

When we are able to keep focused in our work as catechists so that we see the broader picture of what we are engaged in, namely, **planting roots and giving wings,** we

can be energized to keep at it. We can more easily realize that hope must be nurtured to be sustained. Our
encouragement and affirmation can lure our students to
try harder, reach farther and believe more strongly in
themselves and others.

Hope for the future is an essential ingredient of Christianity. Remember the words of Peter spoken to the
crowd right after the first Pentecost:

> . . . this is what the prophet spoke of:
> In the days to come — it is the Lord who speaks —
> I will pour out my spirit on all (hu)mankind.
> Your sons and daughters shall prophesy,
> your young men shall see visions,
> your old men shall dream dreams.

(Acts 2:16–17)

Already at the very beginnings of the church, we see
the need for hope that reality can be transformed and
that the world can be a better place for everyone. Every
now and then, it can be encouraging for us to reflect on
those moments when we see some of our students be-
lieving in themselves a bit more, growing in confidence
of their own abilities, and even delighting in discover-

ing and learning something new. These are the moments that help to "make it all worthwhile."

One more word about wings. They not only help one to fly, but they protect as well. Wings are a metaphor for God's constant love for us. As we encourage our students, we are doing much more that building self-confidence; we are giving them an experience of love. In our love for our students, we are making present God's love for them. The psalmist speaks eloquently of this awareness:

> How precious, O God, is your constant love!
> We find protection under the shadow of your wings.

> (Ps 36:8)

Yes, education has a transforming aspect to it, and it can be a source of empowerment. When done well, with care and intention, teaching contributes much to transformation and empowerment. The following poem describes that part of teaching which is **giving wings**:

> Appollinaire said, "Come to the edge."
> "It's too high."
>
> "Come to the edge."
> "We might fall."

"COME TO THE EDGE."
And they came.

And she pushed them.
And they flew.

Teaching can't get much better than that.

Reflection Questions _____

1. Can you recall a specific incident in which your students really "got it"? Or one in which a student truly felt good about herself or himself? You may wish to pause for a moment to feel grateful for these moments.

2. What do you think precipitated these incidents?

3. Describe any "Aha!" experiences you have had while teaching.

Four

IMAGING OURSELVES, IMAGING GOD

Our image of ourselves has everything to do with our image of God. If our images of self are unhealthy it is all the more difficult to have healthy images of God. A healthy self-image makes it possible to believe that we are, indeed, the *Imago Dei.* Some have said that we live by images. If we think of images as the representations we have of ourselves, our world, and our God, it is probably correct to believe that we live by images. The more vivid the image, the more our lives are influenced by it. Consider the following passage and the images presented in it. Yahweh addresses Jeremiah:

"Get up and make your way down to the potter's house; there I shall let you hear what I have to say." So I went down to the potter's house; and there he was, working at the wheel. And whenever the ves-

sel he was making came out wrong, as happens with
the clay handled by potters, he would start afresh
and work it into another vessel, as potters do. Then
this word of Yahweh was addressed to me, "...can
not I do to you what this potter does? — it is Yahweh who speaks. Yes, as the clay is in the potter's
hands, so you are in mine...." (Jer 18:1–6)

Do the images say anything to you about your own relationship to God? Your own relationship to your students?
Most likely the images in this passage evoke deeper
meanings than would most philosophical or theologi-
cal discourse. Images can enrich us because of the deep
feelings and connections they call forth in us.

Partaking in the Dance of Spirituality ————————

Images are products of the imagination. We nurture our
imagination by saturating it with a variety of experiences,
both cognitive and affective. This is to say that we need
all kinds of experiences in our lives — those that are sen-
sory, aesthetic, and intuitive, for example, in addition to
the cognitive experiences. We need experiences of the
heart *and* the head. The imagination, then, preserves our
zest for life.

The longer we live, we come to realize that we have to balance our lives with play *and* work, and that both of these require that we rest, too. Spiritual writers call this the dance between action and contemplation. Spirituality is lived out between these two poles of our experience. However much we are tempted, we really can't live totally active lives without some space to be still and focused. Nor can we live totally at rest with self and God. We must live our lives between *being* and *doing,* otherwise we can "burn out" or get "stuck." Some spiritual writers describe these experiences as having reached an "impasse" where we feel there is no way out to escape from a situation that we find unbearable or boring. If left unattended these feelings can lead to a lack of assurance, or doubt about self and others. In such situations, spiritual writers and psychologists tell us that the only way out of such a rut is through an "imaginative shock." This is because reasoning alone will not work; we must let go of trying to control everything in our lives and allow ourselves to be open to mystery. To put it another way, change will come about when we allow ourselves to enter into a right-brain mode where our feelings, intuition, and imaginative explorations reside. This is the place of contemplation.

How does this all affect our work as catechists? We will only be as effective as teachers as we are integrated as persons. If we are bored with life, we will be boring teachers. We must make an effort to celebrate the ordinary.

Celebrating the Ordinary _____

We face the following challenges for ourselves:

1. *The challenge to cultivate wonder and appreciation for the ordinary.* We can put on a "new lens" which will allow us to see daily activities from a new perspective. Eating can be a routine or a source of pleasure; bathing can be a mundane necessity or a luxury, listening to others can be an interruption or a moment of grace; being home alone can be depressing or a time of relaxation in which to daydream, listen to music, or do whatever one pleases, etc. These activities can be sources of renewal, familiarity, anticipation and amazing discovery — here is something newly discovered that was always there!

2. *The challenge to cultivate receptivity to ordinary life.* If we are constantly seeking something new or exciting we can miss the magic of daily life. Celebration of daily experience provides opportunities for "mindfulness." We are better able to be engrossed in living the fullness of the moment.

3. *The challenge to cultivate practice in care-taking skills.*

If we "take care" with matters of our daily life, we become more competent in them and we grow more in reverence for life. Reverence brings about a deep, serene joy. And this joy will surely spill over into all of our work as catechists. Joy is contagious.

Image Building _____

We face the following challenges for our students:

1. *The challenge to help students believe in their own goodness.* This is so basic that at first glance it seems silly to mention it. Yet, research shows that many young people have negative images of themselves. In our society, self-worth has too often become identified with externals such as physical looks, material possessions, productivity that is measured in dollars and cents, and external factors of popularity. In our classes we can help students to realize that they are good because they are created in God's image and likeness. The words of St. Paul are a helpful reminder:

> We are God's work of art, created in Christ Jesus to live the good life as from the beginning (God) had meant us to live it.   (Eph 2:10)

2. *The challenge to help students recognize the goodness of God's creation.* This includes the human and nonhuman world. The world is in trouble — even the youngest of students realize it. The depletion of the ozone layer, pollution of water sources, destruction of the rainforests, pervasion of violence on our streets and in our homes, and the ruthless killing of people around the globe are daily brought home to youth through our high-tech media. Care and reverence for God's creation must be fostered at every opportunity. Children who have been taught to care for things find it easier to care for others.

3. *The challenge to help students live in hope for the future.* The confusion, frustration and impatience of being young can be demanding. But it can be a time for personal and social transformation. The work of maturing takes time, as the writer Morris West suggests: "We are like a tree whose whole life is implicit in a tiny seed, but which must grow each year into a new shape and a new fruitfulness."

In the person of the catechist, students have an image of a caring person who loves them irrationally, that is, unconditionally. As catechists we can *sustain our enthusiasm* by disciplining our minds and cultivating our senses so that we can develop our own *imaginations with room for the spiritual.* Then when we look out over our classrooms we will see not only who and what is there, but how to respond with love, truth and justice. And because we are graced, we will be able to show our students how to see the spiritual possibilities present and hidden in forms and events that are often taken for granted — to be able to see in faith, through our and their imagination that:

> . . . nature is never spent;
> There lives the dearest freshness deep down
> things;
> And though the last lights off the black West went,
> Oh, morning, at the brown brink eastward,
> springs —
> Because the Holy Ghost over the bent
> World broods with warm breast and with ah!
> bright wings.

Such an atmosphere surely makes it easier to image oneself as the *Imago Dei* — catechist or student.

A Parable

There are many versions of this parable, but they all suggest the same meaning. This version is offered as a summary of this chapter. Perhaps you can carry it in your heart and think about it when you reflect on your teaching.

A man found an eagle's egg and put it in the nest of a barnyard hen. The eaglet hatched with the brood of chicks and grew up with them.

All his life the eagle did what the barnyard chicks did, thinking he was a barnyard chicken. He scratched the earth for worms and insects. He clucked and cackled. And he would thrash his wings and fly a few feet into the air.

Years passed and the eagle grew very old. One day he saw a magnificent bird above him in the cloudless sky. It glided in graceful majesty among the powerful wind currents with scarcely a beat of its strong, golden wings.

The old eagle looked up in awe. "Who's that?" he asked.

"That's the eagle, the king of the birds," said his neighbor. "He belongs to the sky. We belong to the earth — we're chickens."

So the eagle lived and died a chicken, for that's what he thought he was.

(Anthony De Mello, *Song of the Bird*)

What does this story mean to you?

Reflection Questions _____

1. Some images of being a catechist could include the following:

   - potter
   - sower
   - midwife

   Do any of these images describe the way you feel about your own work as a catechist? Why?

2. Can you think of any other images that might describe your role? Why?

3. Do you think it would be helpful to remind yourself of any of these images as you prepare to meet your students?

Five

JOURNEYING TOWARD GOD

When you become a catechist, you begin a journey that is filled with surprises. Part of the surprise is the discovery that you are not making the journey alone. You have many companions, and some of them are the students you teach. Just as we require food for our human journey, so too do we require companions. The word "companion" is derived from "com" (with) and "panis" (bread). Companions are persons with whom we share bread for the journey. Our co-workers and the students we teach are our companions in a special way because in our search for God we become bread for each other. We are nourished and strengthened by each other. And the recognition of this gives us gladness:

> Happy are the people whose strength is in you!
> whose hearts are set on the pilgrims' way.

> (Ps 84:5)

As catechists, the journey we are on is really a pilgrimage. It is a journey to a sacred place that we are making during the course of human life on earth. Those who have made a pilgrimage realize that it is the *making* of the journey that is transforming and not the *arrival* at the final destination. Our work as catechists, then, is a part of that journeying process towards God in which we are bread for each other on the way.

Teaching as Ministry

In an essay on religious education entitled "Enfleshing the Word," Edward Robinson wrote the following:

> The French philosopher Gabriel Marcel, in a beautiful image, spoke of the infinite possibilities of grace "scattered like pollen on the summer air." But there can be no fertilization until that pollen reaches the flower that is ready and able to receive it. There can be no revelation until the Word reaches those who have ears to hear and eyes to see. And it cannot do this until it is embodied, until it is given expression, and that not once and for all, but continually anew in each generation. (*Religious Education*, Vol. 81, No. 3, p. 362)

How similar this description of the process of teaching is to one that comes from another part of the world. In the southernmost tip of Mexico, there are thousands of Indian communities that dot the Chiapan countryside. In the native language of Tzeltal, the word for *catechist* translates as "one who harvests the word of God present in the community, then spreads it once again." Both passages cited above point to the fact that each generation needs its own teachers. Each community must raise up its own leaders who will minister to its needs. Teaching religion is one such ministry.

There are many definitions of ministry, but all of them share the following characteristics: *ministry is doing something in public, for the coming of the reign of God, on behalf of the community; it is a grace, and it has its own identity and structure.* Teaching religion is a ministry because it fulfills these criteria.

1. *Teaching is doing something in public.* Teaching is never a private affair. As we saw earlier, teaching draws on the richness of our Christian heritage to help students better understand how God functions in human life, and how we are related to God, self, others and the world. Religion is practiced in community.

2. *Teaching is doing something for the coming of the reign of God.* This points to the transformative aspect of teaching. It is that part of teaching which gives *wings* to the

learners to rise above the *status quo* and to change struc-
tures and concrete realities whenever necessary so that
God's justice might prevail.

3. *Teaching is doing something on behalf of the community.* Most of human life is quite ordinary. And most
people spend most of their time doing ordinary things.
But the ordinary is limited. There are some in the community who are called to see the extraordinary in the
ordinary. Catechists are such persons. The community
entrusts its young people to those who are called to point
to the extraordinary in the ordinary (to point to God's
presence in the world). And many adults also recognize
that catechists can be catalysts for their own exploration
and growth in faith.

4. *Teaching is a charism with its own identity and structure.* As we explored earlier, those who teach do so with
intention. Teachers craft their lessons so that they are
whole works. Each lesson has a beginning, middle and
end. And each lesson has a purpose or objective. In religious education, the purpose and/or objectives are clear:
a catechist teaches in the name of the community, for
the good of the community.

The Joy of Being a Catechist
A True Story

It was a bright, sunny morning, and the air was delightfully crisp. As I crossed the bridge over the wide bend of the river, I could see for miles. It was indeed a beautiful autumn day. Since it was Saturday, the traffic was unusually light, so I arrived early at the parish that was hosting the day-long workshop for catechists. "Would anyone be there this early?" I wondered, as I glanced at my watch. The first session was scheduled to begin in an hour and a half. As I ascended the steps I realized that I was not the first to arrive. The meeting hall was already set up. The janitor was giving the very clean floor another going over with a large mop. The whole room seemed to say, "Welcome!" There were tables arranged with sample materials for various grade levels. The coffee pots were already perking, and a large table was laden with an assortment of muffins, bagels and cookies.

As I entered the hall a voice called out to me, "Good morning! And welcome to St. Joan's Parish!" I was pleased to recognize the Director of Religious Education who had been a graduate student of mine more than ten years ago. As usual, Wendy was wearing a big smile. "You look wonderful," I said. "How long has it been since we last saw each other?" She was quick to reply, "About five years, I think. I feel wonderful, and I am so happy to be able to host this meeting." As we spent a few minutes catching up with each other, Wendy's energy seemed to increase as she described her work at the parish. "How long have you been working in religious education," I asked. Without any hesitation she replied, "twenty-two years — and it seems I started only yesterday." That was easy to understand given Wendy's enthusiasm for her work. While we were speaking, people were beginning to gather, and we both made gestures to greet them. "Before you begin speaking with some of the participants, I want to introduce you to someone special," Wendy said. A tall, young woman in her mid-twenties was walking directly toward us. As she approached, Wendy put her arm around her and said, "This is my daughter, Melissa. She just finished graduate school and started a new job." Melissa smiled and said, "Yes, I graduated with an MBA and now I am studying in a whole different field because of my new job as a DRE in a small parish." "Good for you," I said. "And congratulations, too. What made you decide to leave the world of business for parish work? It can't be the salary," I teased. Melissa was quick to respond. "Not at all. As I was getting closer to looking for a full-time job, I was flooded with memories of my mother who worked as far back as I can remember. I recall how each morning she would be filled with such excitement and eagerness to get to work at the parish even though she put in such long days that included raising us kids and keeping house. The more I interviewed for jobs, the more I was drawn to those images of my mother who still loves her work. And it became clear to me that I wanted to do work that would make me as happy as she is. So I decided to become a DRE." I noticed that Wendy was glowing as she listened to her daughter. "What a wonderful compliment to you, Wendy," I said. "How hopeful to see a new generation entering the field. Now we have mothers and daughters working side by side as catechists." "It's just that I love my work so much," Wendy replied. "It is such a joy to work with the catechists, parents and children." And I knew she meant it.

As we each moved to greet the arriving catechists, I was aware of how inspired I was by this conversation. Joy is contagious, and those who answer the call to teach are sure to know *the joy of being a catechist.*

Ministry and Vocation ————————————

There is but one vocation for Christians, and that is the call to holiness. There are many ways to live out this calling. Catechists respond in faith to the calling to serve the community through teaching and witness. To be a catechist is at once a *gift, a promise,* and *demand.* It is *a gift* because it can give us pleasure and joy to serve God and the people of God through the ministry of teaching. It is *a promise* because our teaching brings hope to the community, "and this hope is not deceptive, because the love of God has been poured into our hearts by the Holy Spirit which has been given us" (Rom 5:5).

And it is *a demand* since our work with our students reminds us that we still have much to do. Like St. Paul, our vocation reminds us that we have not won the race, but we are still running, and so we "strain ahead for what is still to come...racing for the finish, for the prize to which God calls us upwards to receive in Christ Jesus" (Phil 3:13–14).

Reflection Questions _____

1. What does it mean to you to know that you are truly participating in the ministry of the Christian community?

2. How does it make you feel to realize that for centuries people like you have been doing the work of catechesis, and that you are now carrying on this tradition of ministry to God's people?

3. Consider some ways in which being a catechist nourishes your own spirit as you journey toward God, e.g.,

- by giving you hope
- by deepening your faith
- by giving you joy
- by _____

EPILOGUE

Our work of teaching daily reminds us that we are building the future. Our work of catechesis is contributing to the renewal of the Christian community as we move into the third millennium. We work in confidence that "the promises of the Lord can be trusted; they are genuine as silver" (Ps 12:6). The promises of the Lord carry us and they fill us with confidence for the future.

> Once more there will be poured on us
> the spirit from above;
> then shall the wilderness be fertile land
> and fertile land become forest.
>
> In the wilderness justice will come to live
> and integrity in the fertile land;
> integrity will bring peace,
> justice will give lasting security.

> My people will live in a peaceful home,
> in safe houses,
> in quiet dwellings. . . .

(Is 32:15–18)

We can take hope that in a world threatened by ecological disaster and economic bankruptcy, in a society imbued with too much materialism, and amidst systemic injustice, people like us still gather to celebrate our lives and vocation, and to worship God, source of all compassion and power, who is the Bread of Life to satisfy our hungry hearts. St. Paul reminds us that "From the beginning till now the entire creation . . . has been groaning in one great act of giving birth" (Rom 8:22). As catechists, we are midwives helping to give birth to a New Creation. May we continue our journey nourished by our faith and hope as we pray to God in the words of Pope John XXIII:

Renew your wonders in our time
and give us a new Pentecost.

AMEN!

A Catechist's Prayer

O Gracious God, You are beyond my imaginings
    but I know that you are here with me.
Be with me as I teach your children.
Fill my heart with your Spirit
    so that I may be true to your Word.
Give me courage to proclaim your love
    to the joyful and the hurting.

O Holy One, bless my students
    so that they may receive your gifts with gratitude.
Keep them open to wonder
    and aware of your love
So that created in your image
    they may reflect your grace.

I ask this in the name of Jesus the Christ. Amen

Published by Resurrection Press

Spirit-Life Audiocassette Collection

Hail Virgin Mother   *Robert Lauder* $6.95
Praying on Your Feet   *Robert Lauder* $6.95
Annulment: Healing-Hope-New Life   *Thomas Molloy* $6.95
Life After Divorce   *Tom Hartman* $6.95
Path to Hope   *John Dillon* $6.95
Thank You Lord!   *McGuire/DeAngelis* $8.95
Spirit Songs   *Jerry DeAngelis* $9.95
Through It All   *Jerry DeAngelis* $9.95

Resurrection Press books and cassettes are available in your local religious bookstore. If you want to be on our mailing list for our up-to-date announcements, please write or phone:

Resurrection Press
P.O. Box 248, Williston Park, NY 11596
1-800-89 BOOKS